"Does God still love me?"

Letters from the Street

Sr. Mary Rose McGeady

Covenant House

DEDICATED
to the 1,000,000
homeless children
who slept on America's streets last year,
scared, cold, hungry, alone,
and most of all, desperate to find
someone who cares.

Copyright 1995 by Sr. Mary Rose McGeady

ALL RIGHTS RESERVED
PRINTED IN THE UNITED STATES OF AMERICA
FIRST EDITION

Table of Contents

Introduction

*"Their hearts have
only one question."*

They come to me every day in droves, a nameless, faceless army — the most lost and alone citizens in America.

In a better world, in a better time, under better circumstances, these lost vagabonds who knock on my crisis shelter door in the cold of night would be doing other things. Like sitting in a 4th grade classroom. Playing softball on a high school team. Or eating dinner around a big dinner table filled with conversation and people who loved them.

Instead, these kids (yes, kids) are eating food out of dumpsters, or sleeping in alleyways. Trying desperately to live in a world where no one loves them. And all too often dying there too.

They are America's street kids. And this is their story.

It would amaze you, I think, if you stood in the doorway of our crisis shelters, and watched them file inside at night (it's a long line — 1,200 are with us each and every night.)

When they come to us, they are full of questions, the type no child should ever have to ask. "Is it safe here," a 14-year-old girl asked me just last night. "I'm scared ... I don't know where to go ... I don't know what to do," her eyes said. It hurt hearing her and seeing her suffer like that. It always does....

The other questions are just as painful to hear: "Can I have something to eat ... I haven't had a good thing to eat in days," a 17-year-old boy asked me last night. "Can I sleep here? Where can I sleep?" another kid asked an hour later. I think she may have been twelve.

These questions come easy to them. They are the questions that a street kid asks every day, minute to minute.

But what gets to me is the question they don't ask. The one that hides deep in the eyes they turn away from you. The one that shows in nervous fingers. This is the question that comes from living a lifetime of days when you can't seem to do anything right.

It is: "Does God still love me?"

The kids would never say that out loud. Very few of them ever talk about God. They don't know enough yet, and their minds and mouths are too preoccupied with the other questions: "Is it safe here?" "Can I have something to eat?" "Where can I sleep?"

But their hearts have only one question: "Does God still love me?"

And their hearts look to me and to the other adults at Covenant House for the answer to that question. I don't think the kids think much about the theological idea that God lives in every one of us. With them it's more instinctive. All I know is that when they look at me and I see that question, I feel the incredible burden of standing in for our Lord. And I know our Lord is counting on me to say, "Yes! Heavens, yes! I love you!" to those scraggly, hungry, angry children of the streets.

In this book I will tell you the stories of some of the kids who've most touched my heart at Covenant House.

Because I want you to feel, and see, and know what their lives have been like, I have told their stories chronologically — through letters I wrote to friends and supporters who share this life-saving mission with me.

Some of these stories will break your heart, others might make you want to cheer. But most of all, I hope you'll get a sense of how much these kids need an answer to that question. And how much the answer depends on you and me.

I think their story will amaze you. I know you will never, ever forget it. They are, after all, just kids....

Sister Mary Rose McGeady
June 9, 1995

Chapter 1

"Does God still love me?"

June 10, 1994

"I'm not afraid, Sister," Michelle said. "Really I'm not."

Her eyes had that look that the dying sometimes get ... a serene gaze that can seem close to angelic. That's how I knew she truly meant what she said.

I took her frail hand and pressed it to my heart.

She had lost so much weight, her hands were as light as birds' wings. I felt if I didn't hold on, they could just flutter away, towards heaven.

She smiled at me, a smile that could light up a room. That's what the rest of the kids at Covenant House remember about Michelle the most. She was always ready with a smile.

"Sister? Can I ask you a favor?"

"Ask away," I replied, my throat sore from holding back tears.

"Will you be with me when I die? Just like this, holding my hand?"

"You can count on it."

Michelle was already HIV positive when I met her.

That was back in 1990. She showed up at our door late one night — a scrawny, raven-haired beauty with deep-set eyes and an infectious laugh.

But the symptoms, those horrible symptoms of AIDS, had already begun to eat away at her....

Sometimes she had night sweats and cried out in her sleep. When she woke up in the morning, the sheets would be soaked all the way through.

She had a hacking cough that never left her. And there were dry patches on her skin that nothing could seem to cure.

We fed her and clothed her and loved her, just like we do all our kids. Only this time, it was a little different.

Because there was no escaping her fate. The kids knew it, I knew it, our staff knew it.

Sooner or later, Michelle was going to die.

There were so many things she wanted to know about death and dying — questions that have challenged theologians and philosophers since the beginning of time.

Questions that, often, I didn't quite know how to answer.

"Sister, why did God give me this disease?"

"Sister, does God accept drug addicts in heaven?"

"Sister, does God still love me? Did God *ever* love me?"

The best I could do was tell Michelle what I believe: that God's love and forgiveness are limitless. And always.

That when she left this earth, she would leave pain and suffering behind. That the unconditional love she never received from her parents would be found in the tender embrace of a loving God.

When I told her these things, she nodded sagely.

"You know, that's just how I thought it would be. That's why I'm not scared to die. I think heaven is going to be a wonderful place, where I never feel lonely or sad.

"You know what I think heaven will be like, Sister?"

"What?" I asked.

"Like living at Covenant House."

We buried Michelle just a few weeks ago. I wish you could have met her, and gotten to know her as we did. I think you would have liked her. I know you would have....

A lot of people condemn kids like Michelle for contracting the HIV virus. They think we should put them behind closed doors and pretend that they don't exist.

But that's just another way to reject them for doing what they have to do in order to survive.

Some contract HIV by prostituting themselves in order to buy their next meal. Others risk infection every time they get high. But they do it anyway.

Because that's the only way they can cope with the horror of life on the streets ... and the knowledge that they have been cast aside by the very people who were supposed to love them without judgment or reservation.

Well, there's one place they can come where they

will never be cast aside. Michelle called it "heaven on earth."

The building's a little old and falling apart in some places (some would say the same of its President!). But as long as both Covenant House and I are still standing, we will welcome every one of God's children with open arms.

If you had looked into Michelle's eyes and seen the light of hope and trust that shone there in her final days on earth, you would have welcomed her into your heart as well. I know you would.

Despite her suffering, Michelle never gave up hope. Before her last visit to the hospital, she was making plans to enter nursing school. After all she had been through, her fondest wish was to devote her life to helping others.

And I believe that she did just that.

You know, the kids put together her Memorial Service themselves.

They read poems by Maya Angelou and Karen Johnson. They told stories. And sang songs. One was by a singer named Eric Clapton. The kids tell me he wrote it right after the tragic death of his young son.

It's called "Tears in Heaven." We all cried when the kids sang it. You couldn't help but cry....

In 40 plus years, I've seen so many miracles. I've seen street kids that many believed were beyond redemption summon up the strength to deal with their pain — and make something beautiful of their lives.

But I'm not sure I've ever known anyone stronger

than that tender-hearted girl who arrived on our doorstep four years ago ... and changed our lives forever.

I'm so grateful that Covenant House was here for Michelle. I spend a part of every day being thankful for the kids that God has sent to us (and even the ones He has taken back).

I know that, in some ways, this was a sad story. But here's the most encouraging thing I can say to you: the fact is, when Michelle had nowhere else to turn, we were here for her. She had a chance to know love and compassion for the first ... probably the only ... time in her life. That's the gift *you* gave to her.

It's the gift you give to all our kids with your kindness, and your support. Thank you, thank you, for caring about our kids.

I never ... we never ... forget the people like you, who make it all possible.

Chapter 2

"I sleep in my pipe."

July 1, 1994

"I'm waiting for my dad. Have ... have any of you seen my dad?"

The tall and skinny scarecrow-kid shifted before us on the streetcorner, fear racing across his face, dirt smeared all over his body.

His speech was slowed and slurred. His eyes dull and empty. At first I thought "drugs," but then I realized it was something else ... the boy was mentally disabled.

He was ... like a baby really. A little boy who had physically grown up into a 16-year-old's body.

"I'm sorry, son, but I don't know your dad. I'd love to help you ... what's your name?"

"Eric."

"Hi, Eric. What do you mean you're waiting for your dad?"

"He's coming back. I hope. 'Cause I'm really hungry."

Eric clinched his hands tightly into a fist, and began to rock back and forth. He was really growing scared.

"Maybe we can help you. Where do you live, Eric?"

"I don't know."

"Do you live in New York City?"

"I don't know."

"Do you live in a city, with lots of streets and buildings?"

"Yeah. Lots of cars."

"When did your dad say he would be back?"

"He just took me for a walk, and then said, 'wait here, I'll be right back.' That was right after he gave me breakfast. But he must be coming back ... right?"

"How long have you been here, Eric?"

"I don't know, but I've been here for awhile."

"Have you slept here?"

"Yeah. I sleep in my pipe. I wish I had my blanket, though, 'cause some nights in my pipe it gets really cold."

"Your pipe? Where is that, Eric?"

Eric pointed to the bridge that runs along the Hunts Point section of the Bronx, and then led us to his "home." Sure enough, hidden in the dirt and squalor of a dark corner, sat a large, old pipe.

"Is this where you sleep, Eric?" He nodded up and down. "Eric, how many times have you slept in the pipe? One time? Two times? Or more?"

"Yeah. I sleep here a lot."

"Eric, what's your last name?"

"Eric."

"No, your other name. Do you have another name? Like, I'm Mary Rose, but my last name is

McGeady. Do you have another name?"

"Just Eric."

"Eric, why don't we leave a note for your dad, and you come back with us to Covenant House. We've got lots of food, and warm blankets, too. Does that sound good?"

The boy-child stood beneath the bridge, tears rolling out of his eyes. Standing there amidst the bedlam of a Friday night in the Bronx, he looked absolutely, positively, incredibly alone.

"I guess so," he sniffed. "But don't hurt me, OK?"

We brought Eric back to Covenant House three days ago. The note, our plea to find his father, has gone unanswered. Our vans have swung by the pipe every day since then, but no one's "home" anymore.

Every time I look at him I want to cry. I mean, my heart aches for every kid who comes to our doors (that's a lot of aches ... 41,000 this year!). But seeing kids like Eric, the children who are mentally disabled and completely unable to fend for themselves ... I think these kids break my heart most of all.

As you and I go to bed tonight, a growing army of kids just like Eric will be out on our streets, absolutely incapable of caring for their basic needs tonight, let alone cope with tomorrow!

Cast adrift by people who are unable or unwilling to care for them, these kids will walk a path very much like Eric's — living in pipes, underground tunnels, any place they can find to survive.

What happens to these defenseless children on the streets is a crime and a disgrace!

It's a good thing our God is a merciful one, because I'm sure He must be terribly angry about what this world does to His children. One expression of God's mercy is the love of people like you.

Thank you. Thank you so very much for helping us be there for Eric that night. And yes, I want to assure you that we're going to do everything possible to help him and care for him.

Already this week, our staff has spent hours checking around trying to figure out who Eric is or where his parents are. And we're going to try to arrange a good foster home or group home for him. Surely, we will be able to find a good and decent place where kids like Eric will be valued and loved, the way every child of God deserves to be valued and loved.

I know one thing — Eric will never spend another night alone in that pipe. Ever! No kid should ever suffer like that!

I know one thing else. Eric's beginning to like us. "The people here are nice to me, Sister Mary. Everyone's nice."

Believe me, the budding love affair is mutual.

P.S. When we brought Eric to Covenant House his first night, he was so dirty we had to use extra-strength mechanic's grease to strip away the layers of dirt on his body. He's so needy ... this wonderful child was never even given a chance to read and write (we'll change that). He needs tons of help. Your prayers will mean a lot!

Chapter 3

"He raped me the first time when I was nine."

She sauntered over to the van, hips swaying in her short white shorts, acting cooler than cool.

But her eyes betrayed her. There was nothing happy inside them.

"Can't get too excited about nothin' when you're out on the street, man," she said.

"It's really good to see you, Bernetta," we said.

We all felt like just throwing our arms around her that first night, but we couldn't. Bernetta was like a skittish colt, and the last thing we wanted to do was scare her off. We were determined to take things slow.

So was she. At first, all she would accept was a cup of lemonade. Then she'd head back to 25th and 9th, the corner of New York City her pimp owned ... all pimps have their "territory" ... and hustle for the rest of the night.

But after a few visits, Bernetta began to stay a little longer. Sometimes, she'd accept a cheese sandwich. And slowly, she began to reveal a little more of herself.

In fact, getting to know Bernetta was like peeling layers off an onion. Including the tears.

"I was already 'broken in' before I got to the city," she said one night, shrugging her shoulders. "My stepdad, he raped me the first time when I was nine.

"Then, whenever he had a little to drink, he'd come creeping into my bedroom, late at night.

"One night, I tried putting a chair up against the door to keep him out. It worked pretty good. But the next day, he was so mad, he smashed that chair to bits, and gave me a black eye.

"He told me if I ever said a word, he'd hurt me bad. Course, he already had...."

Her voice trailed off and she looked inside our van, blinking furiously to drive back the teardrops that hung precariously in the corner of each eye.

She shook her head and swallowed hard.

"After a few years, I left. But I couldn't do nothin,' I never finished school. I couldn't get a job.

"Then I met Freddie (her pimp). He told me there was only one thing in the world I knew how to do, and if I wanted to stay alive on the streets, I better do what I know best.

"I guess he was right," she said, smiling ruefully.

"He's not right, and don't you believe it," we said furiously. We could tell Bernetta was startled. That's why we usually try not to let kids see our anger.

But sometimes we can't help it.

These young girls come from across America to New York City, looking to escape from men ... fathers, brothers, friends, men they loved and trusted ... who have stolen their innocence and shattered their dreams.

By the time they get onto the streets, their self-esteem could fit onto the head of a pin.

Then their pimp tells them that they're good for nothing, that they deserve nothing — and that tiny speck of self worth disappears. Or turns into self loathing. Or gets buried in some deep, secret place.

"Bernetta, we want you to come back to Covenant House with us." Her eyes clouded over with fear.

"I can't. Freddie would kill me. He doesn't even know I talk to you guys. I can't, I just can't."

She began to sob.

"You know where Covenant House is?" we asked. She nodded. "You have one of our cards?" She nodded again.

We touched her hand. "We're going to say an extra prayer for you." (We didn't know then just how much she would need that prayer.)

She smiled through the tears and headed back to her corner of hell.

A few nights ago, the van swung by the corner of 25th and 9th, as we always do. We were really hoping to see Bernetta.

But when we got to the corner and started to pull up to the curb, Bernetta frantically waved us back.

Then she turned on her heel and started walking in the opposite direction.

We pulled away and headed down the street. But we were uncomfortable. And not a little scared. Something was very, very wrong.

So we turned the corner and headed back up the block. When we got there, I saw why Bernetta had tried to warn us off.

Her pimp held her against the wall with one arm. With the other, he punched and slapped her across the face and screamed obscenities.

"Who do you think you're talking to in that van, girl? You want to talk, you talk to me!"

When he spotted the van, he grabbed Bernetta by the hair and dragged her out of sight.

We drove after Bernetta and her pimp, but they escaped down a narrow alleyway.

A few hours later we came back to find her. She was back on the corner. But when we tried to come near, she shook her head and waved us away.

That was a few nights ago.

I think about Bernetta all the time. I think about her sad, empty eyes, and hope that there's still a twinkle hidden deep inside. Mostly, I hope she hung on to that card.

And I pray that God will show her the way to our door.

What I would like to ask this month is that you add your prayers to mine. Pray that Bernetta looks deep into her heart and finds that little speck of self-esteem that I know is buried there.

Pray that she has the strength to take the biggest step of her life ... away from her pimp, away from the street, and onto the steps of the only place in New York City where she can be safe — Covenant House.

I described Bernetta to all our staff members, and asked them to let me know when she arrives, whether it's 6 o'clock in the morning or midnight.

Because I want to be there at the door to greet her, and tell her how glad I am she came.

My friend, I hope she does make it to our door. With your prayers, and a little help from Him, I think she will.

Thank you for letting me tell you about Bernetta. It is so reassuring to me to be able to write you about these kids, and know that you understand.

And that you love and care about them as much as we do.

They feel that love, you must know that they do. In a spiritual sense, it serves as the very foundation upon which they are able to take a risk, and leave the streets behind.

I think about what would happen if Covenant House weren't here for Bernetta ... and for the 1,200 kids who show up on our doorsteps around the country every night. And I shudder. Because we are the only safety net these kids have — and often, their only chance at salvation. Thank God we're here, we're surviving and we have our friends to offer their courage and their unwavering support.

Don't forget that extra prayer for Bernetta. And if you have another minute to spare, pray for the rest of our kids too, won't you?

Chapter 4

*"Please God, help me
find my way."*

July 25, 1994

She came to us on Easter morning, a little, blond, blue-eyed kid from nowhere, wrapped inside blue jeans, a T-shirt, and some torn sneakers.

Everything about her was a mystery at first, an enigma. Even though she ate with us, and walked with us, she shared little and trusted no one. For the entire first day, we didn't even know her name. She wasn't ready to trust us with something so important.

As hard as we fought to get to know her those first few weeks, she made it even harder. She was like a moving target, a shadow who never left an imprint. One minute she was there, sitting quietly in a corner, and the next moment ... poof.

Finding Diane before her counseling sessions was hardest of all. No matter what time of day we scheduled them, she always managed to be late ... five minutes, ten minutes, more. And then, inevitably, she would amble in, softly whispering the same words of apology — "I'm sorry, I was busy doing something else. Sorry...."

After a while, we discovered what that "something else" was.

Diane was praying in a corner of our Chapel.

I never met a kid who prayed more. Many times in April, and May, and June I would pass the Chapel three different times in a day, and see Diane in her corner each time. There, in the quiet, all alone, I could hear her praying to herself, and scribbling little words on a piece of paper.

Slowly, as she became more comfortable with us, she began to join our daily morning prayer service with the other kids (services are optional at Covenant House — we have kids from all religions, and it's always up to the kids to decide whether they want to pray with us. Of course, we're extra-ready to welcome them inside when they decide it's time....).

Things she simply couldn't say or wouldn't say to a counselor, she gladly shared out loud during our daily prayer intentions. The Chapel became her refuge. Day by day, piece by piece, her story began to spill out....

> *Please, God ... do you think you could pray for my little brother, God? He is so young and so scared, God, he could really use your help. You know why, God, she said one day.*

> *Please, God, do you think you could pray for my mother, God? She's a prostitute and an addict ... please help her with her addiction ... and please help her love me, she said another day.*

> *Please, God, please help me find my*

> *way too. I'm an addict too, God, she finally*
> *said one day. I really need your help too,*
> *God.*

Every single day, Diane would also write down a prayer on a piece of paper, and place it in our prayer jar on the altar, which is reserved for prayers that kids don't want to express out loud.

I read her prayers at regular intervals, so I could pray for those intentions. Diane always wrote prayers such as:

> *Jesus, I love you. Help me be good and*
> *help me stay off drugs today. Let me and*
> *my little brother live a good life. I love him*
> *so much. Thank you so much for loving me.*

No day ever passed without Diane placing a prayer in that jar. Sometimes she would fill it with four or five different intentions. The prayers were almost never about herself.

Slowly but surely, talking to God and through God in our Chapel, she helped us all piece together the puzzle of her life.

And she began to trust.

It wasn't easy for Diane to reach out. Many times she cried to me, "I don't know how long I can take it anymore, Sister ... I can't take it."

But she wouldn't let herself give up. Over time Diane went through therapy for drug addiction. She worked hard at separating herself from those who could lead her away from her goals. And she never stopped saying thank you. "Thanks so much for being there and praying with me, Sister," she'd say. "It's you and God that deserve all the credit," I'd say.

After completing our addiction therapy program, she got a job, and then two jobs, and also enrolled in trying to become a lifeguard. I sometimes thought that she was biting off more than she could chew, and I let her know that. But she just smiled — "God and I know what we're doing, Sister," she'd say. "Don't worry."

Then, two weeks ago, she announced that she was leaving. "I'm going, Sister," she said. "It's time to build a life." And just as quickly as she came, our little dove was gone.

I spoke with her again an hour ago, when she stopped by to visit me. She is now a lifeguard, still working two jobs, still dying to stay clean and make it. She has her own apartment, and will begin college this fall, thanks to some financial aid she obtained with our help. "I'm on my way, Sister," she said.

"I'm so very, very proud of you," I said.

"I'm going to the Chapel and talk to God for a minute. Want to come?" she said.

"I'd like that," I said. "I'll see you in a minute."

I've never been more proud of a kid. Or of you. I mean, you're the one who helped make this beautiful story possible. If it wasn't for your help, there wouldn't be a Covenant House where kids like Diane can escape their aloneness and terror on the street, and find a second chance.

I think Diane said it best on the last night before she left ... "I was on the street for a long time, Sister, and I was so scared. Even though I knew I would be abused by my mother if I went back to her house, I almost did it. *I thought dying a slow death at home would be better than dying a quick one on the street....*"

P.S. I know it can be overwhelming to think of it this way, but ... did you know that there were 1,200 other kids at Covenant Houses all around the country last night? 1,200 other kids, carrying 1,200 other burdens, and trying to make 1,200 other dreams come true (that's a lot of dreams!).

Chapter 5

*"He seemed like such a
nice old man at first."*

August 15, 1994

"Hello? Hello? Please answer me if you're there,"
I said into the phone. It was late at the end of a very
long day and I was just about to leave my office. I was
hungry, and tired, and dying to get some sleep. I was
just about to put the phone down, and then....

"Sister, is that you," the whisper said. "It's me ...
Carol ... in South Carolina. I'm sorry to bother you so
late, but ... but I'm having them again ... those nightmares. I'm ... I'm ..."

Even though I was a thousand miles away, I could
see her face on the other end. I could see the words
sticking in her throat, and the tears beginning to stream
down her face. It really hurt....

"Are the nightmares still the same, Carol?" I said.

"Yes," she sobbed. "They're about him. In my
dreams, I'm with him again ... doing all those horrible
things.

"I can't forget, Sister. I ... just ... can't."

"I know," I said. "I know."

"I mean, he seemed like such a nice, old man at
first," she sobbed, reliving the moment again. "Like a
grandfather. He was like 70 ... he said I could live at

his house ... he said he would take care of me.

"I was so alone, Sister ... I was on the street until I met him ... it all sounded so good. And those first few days were great ... he gave me everything ... money, clothes ... he made me feel great.

"And then ... then he started crawling into bed with me at night ... and doing those terrible things. He began to give me cocaine and stuff to make it easier. He ... I ... he used me ... I didn't have anyplace to go, so I stayed.

"And then pretty soon, I ... I couldn't leave. I needed the drugs. And then ... then he started to beat me, too...."

And then Carol began to wail, the awful, screaming, tortured wail that comes from someone who has fallen into a deep, dark, nightmarish place, where all the escape routes seem closed.

I felt so helpless those next three minutes. Whenever one of my kids is hurting, my first instinct is to throw my arms around them and hug them for awhile. But my arms weren't long enough this time. "I'm here for you, Carol," I kept whispering over the phone. "Please take her in your arms now, God," I whispered to myself.

It had been such a long, uphill climb for her....

Carol had come to us a very lost and exhausted and spent young girl, dressed in tattered jeans and with sad, red eyes that seemed to cry every time she opened her mouth to talk to us.

For her first few weeks at Covenant House, we

couldn't really get her to talk about herself ... who she was, why she was here, where she came from, how we could help her. The only words she spoke, she cried out unconsciously in her nightmares, which crept up on her while she was vulnerable and alone at night, unable to run away.

"You don't want to know about me," she'd say. "It hurts too much," she'd say. "I ... I can't talk about it."

Finally though, one night after another nightmare, her lonely pain got to be too much, and she began to open up. She came from South Carolina, but she had to run away, because both her parents beat her. "They were on drugs," she shrugged while she told us. "I guess they couldn't help it," she said.

Frightened for her life, unable to stand the abuse any longer, she had run away to the big city two years ago when she was only sixteen. Penniless and alone, she soon began to sell the only worldly possession she had that anyone seemed to care about — her body.

Then, one night, she met "him."

Frankly, that might have been the last sad chapter in Carol's life. Every year, thousands of kids just like Carol are taken in and destroyed by awful people like this.

But then a miracle intervened in Carol's life. She ran away from him, and found Covenant House. And you.

Thanks to you — thanks to your love and your prayers and your help — we've been able to turn this beautiful child's life around. It hasn't been easy for her. For month after excruciating month, Carol had to go through therapy and countless hours of counseling. But slowly, and surely, she began to face up to the nightmares that lurked inside her.

And we were able to place her with her grandmother back in South Carolina, who has committed to doing all she can to help her grandchild.

It's not over. The nightmares still come sometimes (although they are getting less and less frequent, thank God). And the phone still rings here occasionally (we've told her to call us anytime — anytime — she needs help). But with your prayers, and her grandmother's infinite kindness, and God's help, she's making it back. She's going to make it ... I know it.

"Thanks for letting me call you, Sister," she said before she hung up the phone. "And please ... don't stop praying for me, OK?" she said. "I really need those prayers."

"I won't," I said. "I promise."

I had to write you this letter tonight. I mean, I had to write you right away, and thank you. Carol's story is a reminder to you and me ... a vivid reminder of all the good and wonderful differences you make in our kids' lives.

I can't say it often enough. YOU REALLY DO MAKE A DIFFERENCE!!! Of all the questions I get asked by friends when I meet them, the one I'm most often asked is — "How successful is Covenant House? How many kids do we save?"

Whenever I hear that question, I think of kids like

Carol. The simple truth is, every year, hundreds and hundreds of kids just like Carol — kids who are lost, desperate, with absolutely nowhere to turn — find help and hope and a new life, thanks to you.

Imagine ... a child given the gift of life, thanks to you! And when you hear that kid's voice, and see that kid's smile, it's the most beautiful sight and sound in the world.

Chapter 6

*"And what are the strings
attached," she said.*

October, 1994

"It happened one night while I was lying in bed, Sister....

"My stepbrother snuck into my room again. He said he was going to rape me ... he said there was no way I could escape.

"I had heard him bragging to his friends that morning that he was going to try this, Sister. So I had gotten a knife from our kitchen, and hid it under my pillow. I was really, really scared, Sister.

"As soon as he jumped on my bed, I pulled out the knife and screamed. He jumped up and ran out of the room. I pulled the bed next to the door so no one could get in, but I still couldn't sleep.

"I just grabbed some clothes, and climbed out the bedroom window, and ran.

"I've been out on the street for three days, Sister.

"A policeman saw me sleeping on the street, and told me I should come here, Sister.

"I don't have anyplace else to go."

The girl running for her life was barely 16 years old.

"I'm so glad you found us. We'd love to have you stay with us," I said. "We'd all love to help you."

Susanna swiped a few tears from her eyes and looked away.

"Why would you want to do that?" she said. She couldn't bring herself to look at me. Her eyes were like two hands that had touched a hot stove once too often. She wanted to look at me, I think, but she had been burned by people so often, she wasn't about to let it happen again.

"Can you give me a minute and I'll tell you why," I said. "I guess so," she said.

I reached out to gently lead her to a corner of our cafeteria, but she pulled back. She was skeptical of anyone and anything. She was tiny, skinny, angry, desperate, hungry, brooding, and tired, and carried inside her an innate and palpable mistrust of people. There was so much emptiness behind her brown eyes, I wanted to wince.

I had thirty seconds to make my case. If I messed up, she was gone.

"I know what I'm about to tell you may sound a little empty, even corny. But I'm here — we're all here — because we love kids like you. As a matter of fact, I happen to think kids like you are pretty special."

Her pace quickened and her shoulders jerked off to the side. I could see her biting down on her lips, extra hard.

"Susanna, all I'm asking for right now is the chance to show how much we believe in you, and want to help you. We know you've gotten a raw deal, and we want to make it better.

"We've got plenty of beds, and you're welcome to have one as your own. We've got food to eat, and some clean clothes you can have. We've got medicine. And a lot of people who'd like to be there for you ... talk to you ... help you all we can."

"And what's the catch?" she asked.

"There isn't one," I said. "Caring for someone and helping someone isn't about deals or bargains. It's about commitment. We commit to help you and feed you and be there for you as long as you need us. All we ask in return (the eyebrows started lifting about now) is that you do what you can to help yourself."

I learned long ago not to expect much from this little speech we give our kids. Our kids are in too much pain to feel anything at that moment. Promises are cheap, especially to a 16-year-old girl who's had everything stolen from her. Her expression never changed.

"What's in it for you?" she said.

"I think I would have asked the same question," I said. "There's nothing in it for us ... and everything," I said.

"I mean, we don't ask anything of you *except the promise that you'll help yourself.* I know this sounds crazy now, but I know that one day, if you stick with us, you're going to feel much happier and better about yourself. That will be the gift you give us."

For the longest time Susanna stared away. I can only imagine what was playing through her mind, a long-running horror story filled with nights in bed, terrified of falling asleep.

"I think I'd like to stay," she said.

"I'd really like that," I said. "Thank you, Susanna," I said.

Thank you, God, I whispered to myself. I know He was probably smiling too.

P.S. After this first meeting I've described, Susanna agreed to stay on and work extra-hard to pull her life back together.

AND SHE HAS SUCCEEDED WITH FLYING COLORS. Today, Susanna is 19, she has a job, is going to school at night, and has met and married a very nice young man. And these two great kids have made a vow to each other about their child — "he will *never* feel abandoned like we felt ... he will always be loved!"

Chapter 7

*"I really would rather rot
out here than go back to them."*

November, 1994

"My name is David," he whispered that first night we met him. "I don't want to be out here on the street," he said. "I'm afraid I'm going to die," he said.

"But I'd rather die out here on the street, than try to live at home," he said.

He was a little scrawny kid, the tiniest child we'd ever seen from our van. His hands and feet were so small, his features so frail, that he looked like a little mouse under the flickering light of the street lamp. He was the sweetest-looking street kid we've ever met....

"Please don't ask me to come back to your shelter," he told us that first night. "I can't," he said. "I'm sorry," he said. And then he crept off into the darkness.

The second time we met him was a drizzly night two weeks ago, under the same flickering street lamp. We'd been out in the van, looking for him....

"I guess you're wondering why I'm here," he said that night. "I don't have a choice," he said. "My stepfather ... my stepfather is a pervert ... he beats me and does sexual stuff to me, too. Ever since I was 12 (David is 14), he's been getting into bed with me.

"I reported him to the counselors at school, but my

stepfather denied it, and my mom got mad at me. He just kept doing it. And...."

My little friend couldn't finish his story that night. The tears made sure he couldn't....

"We'd like to be your friend. Please come back with us ... we can help you."

"I can't," he said. "I gotta keep running." And he did just that, running away down an alley. We tried calling out to him, but he kept running....

Earlier tonight, because he was so hungry his stomach hurt and so drenched from the rain he needed dry clothes, David dropped by our shelter for a minute.

"I can't stay," he announced the second he walked in. "I gotta go ... gotta keep moving."

As soon as I heard he was here, I raced downstairs to meet him. I was able to catch up, just as he was leaving the building....

"I've been looking for you, David. We all have."

"I know," the little mouse said. "I've been hiding, I've been moving," he said. "Kids like me don't have no choice. We gotta keep moving. I got to go, Sister."

"Please talk to me," I said. "I want to help you."

"No one can help me," he said. He backed up against our brick building as he spoke, so he could lean against it. He felt more comfortable that way, more in control, more able to scan the dark streets that run alongside. Like everything else he did, he did it for a reason.

"Why don't you come inside the cafeteria again with me. For a second. We'll pack you a few more sandwiches for the night."

"I can't do that," he said. "I gotta stand here. No offense, but this way I can see you and everyone else. I gotta make sure no one sneaks up behind me. They're after me," he said.

"Who's after you?"

"Everyone," he said.

"I mean, my stepfather and mother want me back. They say it doesn't 'look good' to be running away. So they got the police to search for me.

"I won't let them get me, Sister," he said. "I really would rather rot out here, than go back to them," he said.

"Then stay with us," I said. "We'll help you."

"I can't," the mouse said, shaking his head. "I know the rules," he said.

"If I stay with you, you'll have to tell my parents you found me," he said. "I'd rather die," he said.

Tears formed in his eyes as he talked. There was nothing — absolutely nothing cynical or meanspirited or chippy about the way he talked. Even though he was just a little kid, he had learned all the rules on the street. From a purely legal standpoint, he *was* right. If he stayed in our shelter, we *would* have to report that to the authorities.

"Maybe we can work out something better," I said. "Please give us a try," I said. "We can help ... maybe we can work out a plan so you can live with another relative. You've got to get off the street, David, before it kills you. We'll do all we can to help you,

I promise," I said.

"But first you've got to get off the streets before something really bad happens."

"Something bad has," he said. "It already has." The tears were beginning to gush out now. I put my hand on his shoulder. He started to turn away, but then froze. He didn't want me to let go.

"It's not my fault, Sister," he sniffled. "But I've got hooked up with some people who aren't that good. I mean, at least they give me a place to stay," he said. "And they give me money for all the stuff I have to do," he said. I knew what the "stuff" was that he was talking about.

"I know it's not your fault, David," I said. "You're a really good person," I said. "But these people ... your pimp ... they're not good, David. They're not good for you," I said.

"I mean, these people are very, very dangerous. And there are too many bad things that can happen to you," I said. "Things like AIDS," I said.

(The idea that I was speaking to an innocent, sweet, sobbing 14-year-old kid about AIDS in the middle of the night made my heart ache. I honestly thought I was going to get ill at that moment. Please help me keep it together, God, I prayed to myself.)

"I can't worry about AIDS," David mumbled softly to the street pavement. "I'm probably going to die anyway," he said. "What difference does it make how it happens?"

He put his hand on my hand, which was still resting on his shoulder, and tried to smile. For a few seconds, we just looked at each other, doing all we could to let the other person know we cared, both of us knowing he'd be gone in a second.

"I gotta go," he finally said. "I'm sorry ... I really wish I didn't have to go," he said. "My pimp is probably mad as it is," he said.

"Stay with us," I tried one last time.

"Maybe next time," he said. "I'll think about it," he said.

"Thanks," he said.

"Don't give up on yourself," I yelled out loud. "Don't give up on him, God," I whispered, knowing that He hadn't.

"I'm never giving up on you, David," I said.

P.S. I'm not giving up on David. No Way! We're going to keep looking out for David, and keep trying to get him to stay with us. And once he does, I'm going to make sure he's placed in the arms of someone who will care for him, and love him — the way every sweet, 14-year-old kid should be cared for and loved. That's a promise I've made to him, and a promise I'm making to you.

Chapter 8

*"I believe Jesus would
confront the problem."*

Vigil, 1994

On December 6th, at 5:30 PM, I'm going to do something that will make America's pimps and pornographers really hate me.

I can already sense the anger they're going to feel that night. I can literally see the contempt that will be etched on every one of their faces.

On December 6th, some of America's most despicable pimps and pornographers are going to want to strangle me. And I can't wait for that moment to arrive....

> *You see, on December 6th at 5:30 PM, me and a bunch of homeless kids are going to march directly across 42nd Street with all its horrors ...*
>
> *... and again hold a very special Candlelight Prayer Vigil on behalf of all of America's kids.*

Please, please understand something about this Vigil right away. I believe that this 60 minute Vigil *will be the most important 60 minutes I will spend this entire year.*

These 60 minutes represent the single best opportunity you and I will have all year to fight back against the terrible people destroying America's children. And although it may be dangerous for me, it's something God has led me to do. *I must do it for our kids.* I absolutely must ... (of course, the kids will be protected and guarded every minute).

Please let me explain what's going to happen at this year's Vigil, and why it's more important than anything I've ever done!

On December 6th, when darkness falls around 5:00, something magical will begin to happen on the corners of 41st Street and 10th Avenue *(and at our other Covenant Houses nationwide).*

One by one, in the cold night air, a small trickle of kids will begin to wash onto the sidewalk outside our shelter. These kids are probably the most disenfranchised kids in the world — kids who are homeless, hurting, scared, unwanted, sometimes bitter. *But they are an inspiration and an example to me.*

As this bunch of kids swells to the tens, and then twenties and finally the hundreds, this army of kids will band together to head out on a journey ... a defiant march to the center of Times Square.

Step by step, kid by kid, the kids will cross 41st Street and then make a right onto 42nd, each of them holding candles of hope and defiance in their hands. Their walk will take them past America's pornography graveyard for kids, past places where kids are bought and sold and ultimately murdered under marquees bearing names like "Show World" and "Girls! Girls! Girls!"

As these kids — our kids! — walk, some of them will pause to look up at the waiting TV cameras (last year's Vigil was covered by all the major news outlets — helping us reach out to thousands of kids and families). I swear you can see God on every kid's face while they march. It's that beautiful....

Finally, they will come to rest at our final destination, the place where so many pimps and pornographers don't want us to be — the *middle of Times Square*. The world center of glitz and glitter. *The national graveyard for America's homeless kids.*

For 60 shining minutes, though, Times Square will belong to you and me and our kids, and no one else.

For one full hour, our kids and our friends (last year they came from as far away as Alaska and California) will stand together and reach out to God, for God. We'll light candles together, and shine them high against the darkness. We'll say prayers and sing hymns together. Our kids will speak up and speak out, bringing cars and their passengers to a standstill. The media, often so cynical, will see and feel the real beauty of our kids.

And each of us at that moment — the kids and friends standing in Ft. Lauderdale, New Orleans, Houston, Atlantic City, Newark, Los Angeles, Anchorage, Toronto, and in Times Square — will all feel God among us and truly inside us.

> *One by one, candle by candle, each of us will be re-staking our claim to areas that have become graveyards for America's kids. On this night, we will stand together, in the*

*shadows of some very angry pimps and
pornographers, and defiantly light a different light in places like Times Square ... a
light of hope, and goodness.*

Please watch over these kids of ours, God, we'll
say. To those kids new to the streets who still have a
chance ... help these kids find us. To those kids sinking
in the quicksand of the street and frantically reaching
out for a lifeline ... help these kids discover us. To
those kids who are walking their final days of a nightmarish teenage death sentence ... help us shower these
kids with our love for as long as they need us.

*I know from experience that our prayers will be
answered that night.* It won't take long. During the
Vigil, lots of kids will see our candles, which hang
over Times Square like that star hung over Bethlehem
that night.

And these kids will come. And be rescued.

And even after we finish our final prayer, and begin
our procession back to the shelter, the light of hope we
leave behind will stay. I know God will see to that.

*Since we held our Vigil across America
last year, God has led an increasing number
of kids to our doors. Since our Vigil last
year, the number of kids coming to
Covenant House has skyrocketed by 10,000
kids ... to 41,000 in all! Imagine ... in the
past year we've helped 10,000 more kids
than ever before. I know our Vigil had*

something to do with that. I just know it....

Now can you see why I believe so passionately in this Vigil? Why I'd rather be in Times Square on December 6th than any other place in the world?

I don't have any naive, pie-in-the-sky illusions about this Vigil. I know that this Vigil will not change the world overnight.

But I do know from experience that our Vigil will begin to refocus people. By standing together in Times Square and in eight other cities nationwide, you and I can again make the media and the world take notice about the plight facing America's children. For sixty minutes, and for days afterwards, you and I will put a huge, don't-think-this-problem-is-going-away micro-scope on a crushing national problem that reaches onto every street, and every home in America.

And I know one other thing. It's something God has called me to do. Being part of this Vigil is some-thing God has called each of us to do.

I believe with all my heart that there is only one question facing each of us in the service of America's kids — what would Jesus do? *And I believe Jesus would confront the problem ... condemn it ... and call his followers to fight it.*

I believe this Candlelight Vigil is a tangible expres-sion of everything that is good and decent and right about Covenant House and our kids. And, I hope that it will speak to the powers of evil and darkness that surround us.

And I believe that your prayers with us will make a

difference. Please, please pray for our kids during this special Vigil. America's children have never needed you more.

Chapter 9

"A manger to our kids."

Christmas, 1994

I feel really sorry for people who don't believe in miracles.

Because I get to see them every Christmas.

You see, on Christmas Eve something incredible begins to happen to our kids at Covenant House. It will begin, as it has every year for the past 25 years, with a knock on our door....

"Hi, my name is Sharon," a 14-year-old girl will say. "I'm all alone," she'll say. "Please ... no one in this whole world loves me," her eyes will say.

When Sharon talks to us this Christmas Eve, she'll tell us how she ran away from home to escape sexual abuse, only to be abused and enslaved by a pimp. She'll tell us how she's hungry. And tired. And completely, utterly lost.

And what she doesn't say through words, her eyes will tell me. When I look into them, Sharon will tell me that she wants more than anything to be an innocent little girl again.

It will be easy to see Jesus in those eyes.

But it won't be the Jesus we commonly think of at Christmas, someone who is universally revered and loved, in long flowing robes. I'll see the Jesus who was a social outcast and outsider, the one who the power brokers of His time thought was immoral and blasphemous. I'll see the Jesus who asked God to take the cup away from Him, and let Him be innocent again.

And I'll see a hurting child, a kid who's given up on miracles (fortunately, God hasn't given up on her).

Minutes after I meet Sharon this Christmas Eve, I'll also meet an angry young man named Michael. "Hi," he'll say standing outside the door. "I'm all alone. My father abandoned me when I was two ... my mother's an alcoholic who kicked me out of the house."

He won't have to tell me he feels utterly betrayed by life, that he feels completely unloved and unwanted. His eyes will tell me for him.

I'll, of course, see Jesus in those dark eyes, too.

I'll see the Jesus who knew that the very people who swore they loved Him were going to betray Him.

When Michael shuffles off to bed that night, he won't know he is walking into a miracle. But I'll know it will happen....

And this Christmas Eve, I'll meet Ryan, a bewildered little boy, not yet 12. "My mother gave me a bus ticket to New York and told me to go live with my aunt," he'll tell me. "But my aunt never came to pick me up at the bus station. I can't find her or my mother."

By the time Ryan makes it to us, he will have been wandering the streets for a week. He will be so innocent and unsure, he won't have the foggiest idea what to do.

I'll see Jesus in the eyes of this frightened little

mouse, too.

I'll see the Jesus who cried out on the cross, "My God. My God. Why have you abandoned Me?"

I'll give Ryan an extra long hug on Christmas Eve. And I'll thank God that the miracle will happen in his life, too.

I'm really not sure exactly how the miracle happens at Covenant House on Christmas Eve. But it does....

Somehow, God comes to Covenant House on Christmas Eve and changes something inside our kids.

It must be a lot of fun for Him. I'll bet that of all the days of the year, God loves Christmas best.

All year long, God watches us here on earth and He must worry constantly. He must worry about what we do to each other. I'm sure He cries for His kids and the way they are mistreated and abused.

But on Christmas Eve, I imagine Him saying to Himself, "Tonight, I'm going to give them a chance to start over again. Tonight, I'm going to shower the world with so much love that they'll have to love each other."

And when He does that, all those lonely, tired, broken kids who come to us on Christmas Eve will be transformed.

Sharon, the 14-year-old prostitute, will be changed.

In her place will be a little girl with red and green ribbons in her ponytails. She'll be hugging a teddy bear as if she were a pre-schooler. When I see her smile, I'll know that for one day at least, she is an innocent little girl again. That she feels a hope she hasn't felt in a long, long time.

Michael, the angry young man, will be changed too.

In his place will be a young man singing "O Come All Ye Faithful" very loudly. He'll have his arms around two other kids and he'll look like he trusts the world again. At the very least, he'll finally know someone cares.

Ryan, the frightened little mouse, will be different, too.

In his place will be a child who feels safe and secure enough to laugh, and to tease one of our counselors about the funny elf hat she is wearing.

Jesus will still be in their faces, but it won't be the same Jesus. I won't see the tired Jesus, the social outcast Jesus, the pariah Jesus, the betrayed or abandoned Jesus.

Instead, when I look in the kids' eyes, I'll see Jesus wrapped in swaddling clothes, lying in a manger. I'll see the baby-faced Jesus of Bethlehem, entering a new world with hope and faith.

And I'll know that God has given our kids another chance — and given us another chance to love them the way He does.

A miracle? I know it is. When all is said and done, at Christmas, this place called Covenant House stops being just a house — but a manger to our kids. A place where miracles are born. The birthplace of rebirths. It is that day, when our vision of faith seems most clear — the simple fact that we see in every kid the repetition of the original Christmas. It's one of the most beautiful things I've ever seen.

Of course, you make it all possible for our kids that day. Your love truly shines like a beacon of hope over this shelter for our kids on Christmas — much like that star hung over that manger in Bethlehem that first Christmas Eve.

The Christmas miracle of Covenant House simply wouldn't happen without you. That's why my first prayer on Christmas morning is always one of thanks that you found us. Always....

God bless you. And may you and those you love enjoy a most blessed Christmas. Our kids and I will be praying for you.

Chapter 10

*"If you ever met them,
you would love them."*

January, 1995

Seventeen-year-old Bobby trudged into Covenant House last winter, freezing inside a wet T-shirt, his body covered with lice. "I've been on the street for six months ... I can't live out of a garbage can anymore ... this ain't living," he told us. Today Bobby is a star in our Rights of Passage program, holding down two jobs....

Nineteen-year-old Richard knows what it's like to see the other side, too. Two years ago he escaped to us from an abusive stepfather, carrying painful scars and an addiction to crack. This summer Richard interrupted his "graduation speech" at Rights of Passage to hand out bouquets of flowers to three counselors who "saved my life...."

Kim's a classic middle-class kid from a middle-class family, who came to us this summer, lost and sobbing and homeless ... and eight months pregnant. A couple of months later, Kim and her two-month-old son stepped into an airplane and headed home, reunited with the parents that had written her off....

Each of these kids came to us this year for a thousand different reasons, but ultimately for one simple one

— they had no place else to go.

And like so many thousands of kids who come to us every year, these kids will make it back to see the other side of life.

They are more than just kids — they are living and breathing and walking monuments to your love, and the miracle that is Covenant House.

And they are the best answer I can ever give to the question I get asked most often by our friends and donors — "How successful is Covenant House?"

It's actually a pretty complicated question to answer.

About four in every ten kids who come to us this year will go on to lead fulfilling and happy lives. (An extraordinary success rate — unprecedented, really — given the work we do and the kids we serve. Thanks for making that possible!)

The others? Well ... about "three in ten" of these boys and girls are literally gone when they get here. Sure, they're breathing in and out, but the look in their eyes, and the deadening blackness in those eyes show they've already given up hope.

Adrift and alone on the street long before they ever discover us, these kids have long since succumbed to the drug dealers and pimps and pornographers who set up shop on our city's streetcorners. We pray for them to stay, we literally beg them. But they can't. If disease or a drug overdose doesn't claim them, then the random violence of the street will. Their pain is manifest and absolute.

We do all we can for these kids. And after we've done our part, we leave them to God, all the time hoping for the best. And we never, ever stop praying for them.

Sometimes ... sometimes a miracle happens in their lives. Every once in a while, I get a letter from a kid I thought didn't have a chance of making it. That's the great beauty and mystery about our covenant — we're here for all of them. Because in our hearts, we are hoping for that miracle.

As for the final "three in ten kids?" These are what I call our "in between kids" — the ones who aren't dead yet, but they're not much better off either. When they come into our shelter, the dying has already started inside them. I cringe inside when I see the pain and fear in their eyes....

We spend a lot of time with these kids. We shower them with love. We literally overpower them with all the kindness we can muster. And then we go farther, providing basics like counseling, job training, and more.

Even with all our help and our prayers, most of these kids don't make it either.

Some learn they have AIDS just when they feel they've gotten it all together. Some fall apart when they lose their last, final link to family. Some just become so exhausted by the unimaginable task of climbing straight up out of their dark hole, that they can't go on any farther.

It is for these kids — those who will rise like a

phoenix out of the ashes and those who will die with the certain knowledge of our love and prayers — that Covenant House exists. Because of you, they have a real chance....

Amidst all the uncertainty of being President of Covenant House (I celebrated my four-year anniversary in September), there is one surety that sustains each of us — the certainty that this is God's work, and these kids are among the most loved of His children.

If you ever met them, you would love them. I know that. They're not really any different than any other kids you may know. They're young, curious, passionate, caring, sometimes annoying, often infuriating, feeling, vulnerable, infinitely loving ... kids.

Most of all, though, what happens to them should not happen.

God will lead 1,200 of these kids into our vigilant arms tonight. It helps me a lot (in fact, it makes facing this awesome task we'll be facing again this winter, manageable) knowing you will be there helping us *again*.

Beyond any possible way of saying it, I am eternally grateful to you and for you for loving them as you do. Without you and your constant prayers and help, we simply could not be here for these kids.

We can only be here for them if you are.

We can only save Bobby, and Richard, and Kim because you care.

Chapter 11

"Sister, what do you do if your mother doesn't want you?"

January 13, 1995

"Good luck, kid," the man yelled as he drove away. "Good luck...."

The young girl stood on the curb, and watched the taillights disappear in the nighttime traffic.

For an instant, she began to lurch forward towards the car, but she caught herself. During the next minute, then two minutes, then longer, she stood transfixed on the curb in front of Covenant House, her eyes closed.

We could almost see her body and soul imploding inside her clothes, retreating deep within herself, searching desperately for some shred of emotional safety.

"Are you okay?" Jim, our security guard, asked her.

Her eyes remained closed and she didn't answer.

"Why don't you come inside?" he whispered. "Why don't you come inside...."

Her eyes flashed open and she turned to Jim with a gasp of fear. "It's okay," he said, "I won't hurt you. Are you okay? You look upset."

Before we could do a thing, the young girl collapsed on the sidewalk in tears and sobs that shook her from head to toe.

It took ten minutes to calm her enough to get her inside Covenant House so I could find out what had happened.

"Who was that man who dropped you off?" I asked her.

"That was my father. I was supposed to live with him, but he doesn't want me."

"Where were you living before?"

"I was living with my mother in Seattle. But she just decided to get married again and she said she didn't want me anymore. She told me I was supposed to go live with my dad. I haven't even seen him in ten years."

"How did you get all the way here to Atlantic City?"

"My mom put me on a bus. My dad met me at the bus station, but he wouldn't even let me go home to his house. He just drove me here and told me to get out.

"What am I going to do now? I'm only 15."

She started to cry again. I realized I hadn't even gotten her name yet.

"What do you do if your mother doesn't want you and your father doesn't want you?" she said. "Where do I go?

"It's all gone. Everything is gone."

The counselors and I enveloped her in a huge hug. There didn't seem to be anything else to do.

We spent that evening comforting her and telling her that she was welcomed and we loved her. I think she believed us in her head, but her heart wasn't listening.

Her heart was still shattering with every passing second.

What *does* a kid like her do when her mother doesn't want her and her dad doesn't want her?

We are going to love her to death here, but no matter how much we try, we can never be her parents.

We'll never be able to say, "I remember your first words," or, "Here's a picture of you when you were just three. You were so cute," or, "Do you remember when grandpa used to bounce you on his knee? You loved that so much. You would just squeal."

All of that is gone for her now. She has lost her past and her family roots.

When her father dropped her off at the curb, he forgot to give her identity. When her mother put her on that bus in Seattle, she forgot to pack her childhood ...

... now it's all gone.

I just can't believe the things some parents do to their kids. Sometimes I want to force-feed them "growing up" pills.

Can you imagine treating a child that way? Can you imagine playing cross-country hot potato with a 15-year-old child? They might as well have thrown her on the trash heap and said, "Oh, well, we're tired of that one."

Sometimes the things I see happening to kids just make me sick. And I hate to say it, but I see things like this more and more all the time. And it's not just parents. It's as if this country has decided to pass on all responsibility for kids.

"Good luck, kid," seems to be the guiding principle.
I'm so glad for Kerri (that turned out to be her name) that you don't feel that way about kids. I thank God every day that you don't feel that way.

P.S. We're trying to find a relative who wants to take Kerri. If that doesn't work, we'll find some other loving home for her. In the meantime, we'll keep comforting her when she cries and we'll try to help her keep her hopes up. I keep thinking, 'This kid is so sweet and innocent. What would have happened to her if Covenant House didn't exist?' Thanks to you, the things I imagine are only thoughts in my mind and not the reality of this abandoned young girl.

Chapter 12

"Please don't cry, Annette," the little girl kept whispering in the pew behind me.

"I can't stand it when you cry."

The two girls sat side by side in the second row of our Chapel, trying desperately to be quiet, and good, and behaved. The older girl was named Sonia. Her younger sister was named Annette. They were little and sweet and scared and 15 and 13 years old.

And they were both homeless.

"Please stop sucking your thumb, Annette," Sonia said, pulling her sister's hand out of her mouth. "It's not nice to suck your thumb in church," she said.

"I can't help it," the 13 year old cried in a baby-like whisper. "My stomach hurts," she said.

"Your stomach always hurts whenever you think about Mommy," Sonia whispered.

"I know," she said. "I can't help it." The tears began to gush out even faster.

It was hard to hear much at all during the final five minutes of our special Chapel service this morning. As always, the kids sang their hearts out at the end, and the final prayers seemed to be the loudest of all. (I don't know what it is about kids, but they always seem to perk up at the end of church, and save their strongest words for then....)

But all I kept hearing were the words of a scared little girl talking to a petrified little sister — "Don't cry, Annette. Please."

I scooted over and sat next to them as the prayer service ended.

"Hi, I'm Sister Mary Rose," I said. "Would you like to talk?" I said.

Sonia nodded her head quietly up and down. Annette sucked her thumb a little harder and started crying a little more.

"My name is Sonia," the older girl said. "This is my little sister, Annette."

"When did you get here, Sonia," I said. "I haven't seen you before."

"We came here yesterday," she said. "We didn't have any choice," she said. Annette nodded her head up and down. Her eyes were really dripping now.

"Why did you leave home?"

"We ... we had to leave," Sonia said. "My mother's boyfriend ... he was doing some really bad things to Annette and me," she said.

"A lot of times when we were in bed, he ... he would...."

Sonia couldn't finish the sentence. She didn't have to. I've been around sexually-abused girls long enough to spot it a mile away.

"Did you talk to your mother about this?" I said.

"We wanted to," Sonia said, "but he said he would

kill us if we talked to Mom. He wasn't kidding either, Sister," she said.

"Finally, though, we told our mom what that guy was doing. Our mom didn't believe us at first. She got mad at us. But then one night she came into my room and he was in my bed....

"She caught him, Sister," she said. "She had to believe us," she said. Sonia choked on each word, barely able to get them out. Annette just looked at the ground, sucking furiously on her thumb, tears gushing out. Both little kids were trembling.

I reached out and hugged them for a minute. "What happened after that," I said.

"My mom kicked him out of the house. But then ... we didn't have any money. So we got kicked out of our apartment. We all went to live in a homeless shelter.

"Then in the morning, when we were wandering around outside, my mother suddenly told us we had to go. She said she had to leave us and find a job. She told us we were on our own."

Annette began wailing again, which sounded absolutely awful with her thumb in her mouth. Sonia reached over and tried to pull it out, but she couldn't. Both of the girls began sobbing even harder.

I swallowed hard and threw my arms around both of them and hugged them for a long, long time. Neither of the girls could stop crying. It was really hard not to cry myself.

I can't stop thinking about these kids. I can't stop thinking about how utterly alone they are, and lost, and searching, and empty. I think there's a reason God sent them to me as Lent approaches. Maybe it's His way of again reminding me what Lent is all about?

I mean, Lent is all about tough questions. It's all about things we must ask ourselves, and reckoning, and looking in the mirror and seeing if we like what's staring back at us.

(I must confess I've never liked Lent. It's not something we're supposed to like, I guess.)

It's not easy spending 40 days staring into the mirrors of our souls, and scrutinizing our relationship with God. It's not easy asking ourselves if we're really being as good as we want to be, as virtuous, as steadfast, as understanding. But it's good for us, I think. Lent is one time when we are very much in touch with God.

Our kids? Kids like Sonia and Annette? I think they understand Lent better than many of us ever will. Our kids live in a perpetual Lent ... a nonstop life of painful reckoning, questioning, excruciating self-examination.

I mean, you and I may give up things these next 40 days by choice. Our kids have spent an entire lifetime giving up things ... things that no kid should ever be forced to give up.

They give up their innocence, unwillingly and violently, because most of them have been forced at a young age to do things no child should ever, ever have to do. They give up their dreams — of feeling safe and secure and surrounded by loving parents. They give up hope — of feeling cared for, nurtured, wanted.

Lent is in their hearts every minute of their lives.

And I think more than any other kids in the world, they have the right to be called the least of His Brethren. Maybe that's one more reason why you and I love them so very much. In their own way, our kids know things maybe I never will. To them, the perpetual pain and reckoning and soul-searching of Lent is all-consuming. And without our help, always....

Maybe more than anything, they explain to us why Covenant House exists? Why we positively, absolutely, undeniably have to be here.

Can you maybe join me in saying a little extra prayer for our kids tonight? Ask God to know the muffled tears Annette cries through her thumb — and even more importantly, to know the tears that Sonia holds back.

And if you can, maybe you could also whisper a prayer for the other 1,198 kids in our shelters tonight too. Each kid in their own perpetual Lent. Each one, desperately hoping we might help them find a way out. As always, it will mean a lot to me if you could.

P.S. I think my kids — our kids — really do belong to God in a very special way. I mean, He knew loneliness, and so do they. He prayed to His Father to be delivered, and so do they. He wondered what God had in store for Him, and so do they.

And when I think about all these things, it just strengthens my belief that these are God's kids, that in some mysterious way He has chosen them, selected them to be His special friends, to be called to suffer with Jesus. Please ... I really hope you will help them, and pray for them this Lent. Thank you!!!

Chapter 13

"When I went home from school that day, my mom was just lying there on the floor," he said.

"I ran over to help her, but it was too late. A big ball of socks was stuffed down her throat. I ... I couldn't do anything to help her," he said.

"I'm so sorry," I said. "That must have been so awful," I said. He nodded gently, and looked away. The tears forming in his eyes said all that he wanted to say.

"What did you do then?" I said.

"I didn't know what to do," he said. "I mean, I was so scared, and I didn't know anyone I could call. I ... I finally just called the police, and I watched them take my mom away. And ... and then I just ran, Sister. I was scared. My mom was the only person in my life who I ever cared about," he said.

"You didn't know anyone else?"

"No," he said. "I mean, there were a couple of people I knew, but there was no one I could live with," he said. "I was on my own," he said.

Greg shifted his weight from one side to the other and stared right at me. There was nothing mean or bitter in his voice, nothing but goodness and tears inside his eyes. Homeless, and all alone at 17, he still exudes a kind of unblinking gentleness you don't see in many kids, or a lot of adults for that matter. He's one of the nicest and best kids I've ever met....

"But how did you ever survive alone," I said. "It must have been very hard," I said.

Greg bit his lip extra hard, and caught himself before he let the words spill out. "It was terrible," he said. "Really scary ... really horrible. The landlord said if I didn't have any money, I couldn't stay in the apartment. So he kicked me out."

"But where did you sleep at night?" I said.

"I slept everywhere," he said. "At the bus station ... in an abandoned house I found. On the street, in a warm alleyway. And sometimes I was able to stay at a guy's house ... a guy who ... a guy who knew my mother," he said.

"Who was this guy?" I said.

"Well ... he's just a guy my mom knew," he said. "He ... he did business with her, I guess," he said.

For the first time in our conversation, Greg looked away, unable to face me. It's not easy for a kid, even a kid as tough and good and strong as Greg, to tell someone else that your mother spent her last few years on this earth being a prostitute. I put my hand on his shoulder and told him I understood.

"My mom was into some bad things at the end," he said. "But she was good," he said. "She didn't deserve to die like that, Sister. She was good," he said.

"I'm sure she was," I said. "We can never take her

place," I said. "But we'd like to help you," I said.

"Thanks," he said. "I really need help," he said. "I mean, it's been really rough trying to live and go to school right now," he said.

"You still go to school?" I said.

"Well ... yeah," he said. "I mean, I always promised my mom I would make something of myself," he said. "And I know how important school is. So I kept going. I've already finished my junior year, Sister," he said. "Call my school, they'll tell you that," he said.

"But ... how were you able to do that," I said. "It must have been incredibly hard going to school, when your life was so hard," I said. (I'll be totally blunt. I couldn't believe what I was hearing! I was in awe! I mean, I don't think I could have done what this kid did. I don't think I could have had his courage or smarts in that situation. I was absolutely blown away!)

Greg looked at me and shrugged. "You just do what you have to do," he said.

I stood there, and stared into his eyes, absolutely stunned by his courage, and his decency. There were a million things I wanted to say at that moment, but I decided to simply say the thing he needed to hear most of all.

"I'm so glad you found us," I said.

"I didn't really find you," he said. "That guy ... her friend ... he dropped me off here," he said. "He said, maybe you people can help me."

Can you help me, Greg's eyes said to me. I've seen my mom murdered, I've slept on the street too long and been in agony too long, and I'm still just a kid and I need someone to care. Will you show me someone cares if I live or die, his eyes said.

I reached out and hugged Greg for an extra long time.

"We're going to help you all we can," I said. "Don't worry," I said.

He is 17, and he's seen his mother killed, and he's walked the streets alone without a friend in the world. If ever I met a kid who's beaten the odds just by reaching our doorway, it's Greg.

He came to us about 30 days ago, but he's touched our hearts for eternity. I think God sent him to me this Easter season for a reason. He's a miracle, an Easter present from God, a real-life, flesh and bones resurrection waiting to happen.

"I really didn't find you," he said. "That guy dropped me off here," he said.

I'm sure Greg doesn't see himself as an Easter present. Tonight, when he puts his head down on a clean, safe pillow, he'll be too tired and relieved to think about Easter and a resurrection that happened almost 2,000 years ago in a place far away.

I mean, it's tough for a kid who's been dying on the street to understand the mystery of His salvation and redemption. Kids like Greg, kids who've spent their entire lives knowing the pain of a lifetime of Good Fridays are consumed with the basic questions — like, "what will happen to me," " why doesn't anyone love me," ... "will anyone ever love me?"

But I see resurrection happening inside him already. He's one of our kids who's going to make it, one of the thousands of kids who will be reborn into a brighter and more promising and loving world thanks to you.

Maybe that's the greatest gift all of us can learn from Covenant House. That we witness Resurrection each and every day....

Thank you so much for helping us be there for Greg, to be part of his resurrection! I mean, you can imagine our joy — and his! — when he slowly begins to rise out of his crucifixion on the street, and find the hope we give to him. There is nothing, absolutely nothing more beautiful in this world....

And you make it all possible. You really do....

That's why, this Easter, as we all give thanks to God for all we have, we will save some of our biggest prayers for you. The simple Easter truth is, if God weren't with us, we wouldn't be here to save and resurrect kids like Greg. God and you. I don't know any other way to say it. Our Easter begins with you.

* Drug or alcohol use. You might notice irrational

Chapter 14

"We all live in a box," he said.

May, 1995

"We all live in a box," the biggest kid said.

"A what?" I said.

"A box," he said.

"How many of you live in it?" I said.

"All six of us," he said.

"Six of you, in the same box?" I said.

"Well, yeah," the oldest boy said, a little embarrassed at the thought. "I mean, it's a big box."

"Yeah, Sister," the littlest one said. "It is pretty big, Sister."

"It really concerns me that you are outside," I said. "Why aren't you home?" I said (although I already knew the answer).

"I don't got a home," the littlest kid said. "My father ... my father beat me," he said. "I had to run ... I was really afraid he was going to kill me," he said.

"Same with me," the middle kid said. "Me too," the big one said. "There ain't no such thing as home," a fourth kid said. "My mom and dad beat me too," another kid said.

The six kids huddled closer together and stared at me, trying not to look too ashamed or embarrassed about how they looked and how they sounded.

They were dirty, and bedraggled, and unkempt, and dressed in rags — and they were infinitely beautiful. Under all the filth and insecurity, I could see six great children.

Six beautiful kids who lived inside a box. I wanted to hug them all.

"It's really not a bad box," the youngest (who looked about 11 or 12) mumbled again. I could tell he felt hurt, and desperately needed my approval.

"I'm sure you make it as good as it ever could be," I smiled back, and patted his little back.

"Yeah, it's a big cement box," one of the middle kids said. "It has some kind of transformer inside, which is great 'cause it gives off heat and keeps us warm at night. This past winter, that really came in handy," he said.

"It really helped in the winter," the little one chimed in again. "Yeah, it really did." His eyes were so beautiful and pure I felt like I was going to cry.

"Do you think I could see this box?" I asked. "I mean, is that O.K.?"

The kids looked at each other, waiting for the oldest boy to make the decision. But the youngest couldn't wait. "Sure, Sister," he said. "It's not far from here."

When we got there, the kids scrambled over a chain link fence surrounding a sort of concrete cavern. I didn't even try to follow them. The idea of a 65-year-old nun trying to climb a fence was just too ridiculous.

The kids stood in front of their box beaming like

elementary school kids showing their teacher an art project.

"It's great," the biggest kid said. He was obviously the leader. "It's dry and warm and even has a fence for protection. So don't worry about us," he said. The others nodded.

I wanted to point out to him how quickly he had climbed that fence and how little protection it really was. But it was the "Don't worry about us" that really got to me.

"You know," I said, "we've got a great place for you to stay tonight, if you don't want to sleep in this box. We've got warm, clean beds, and good food, and clean clothes, and you can take a hot shower. Would you like to come back to our shelter with me?" I said.

I was trying to act cool, because I didn't want them to see how scared and worried I was for them, because that would only make them more scared and worried.

For their part, they tried to act like they didn't hear me. The moment I invited them in, all eyes dropped to the ground, not ready to trust anyone yet, in a world they already knew could never be trusted.

"Well, thanks, but not now," the oldest finally said. "We got it all figured out," he said. "We're like a family. We all take care of each other."

I resisted the temptation to lecture them about their dream world. They probably wouldn't listen ... and they'll learn soon enough on their own.

I just hope they're still alive enough to learn.

I wanted to yell. "YOU CALL THIS A FAMILY!

A FAMILY IS SUPPOSED TO PROTECT KIDS AND HELP THEM PREPARE FOR LIFE!

"NOT ONE OF YOU IS OVER 18. YOU DON'T KNOW ANYTHING ABOUT LIFE YET! BUT YOU'RE GOING TO LEARN.

"YOU'RE GOING TO LEARN ABOUT PIMPS AND PUSHERS. YOU'RE GOING TO LEARN ABOUT PNEUMONIA — AND EVEN WORSE DISEASES. YOU'RE GOING TO LEARN ABOUT HUNGER AND HOW QUICKLY YOU CAN DIE. HAVE YOU THOUGHT ABOUT THAT?

"HAVE YOU THOUGHT ABOUT THE REST OF YOUR LIVES? DO YOU REALLY WANT TO LIVE IN A CEMENT BOX FOREVER? AND IF NOT, HOW WILL YOU EVER GET OUT OF HERE?

"I'LL TELL YOU HOW, BECAUSE THERE ARE ONLY THREE WAYS. DRUGS, PROSTITUTION ... OR DEATH.

"THAT'S IT, KIDS. THAT'S YOUR FUTURE."

I didn't say any of those things. I looked at those bright, hopeful — and hopelessly naive — faces and I asked God to watch over them. I'm sure He will....

"GOD! YOU BETTER WATCH OVER THESE KIDS! AND YOU BETTER SEND THEM TO US BEFORE IT'S TOO LATE!" I prayed.

In the end, I gave the kids sandwiches, some clothes ... and I gave them each a Covenant House card. I promised them we'd be ready whenever they need us.

"Thanks anyway," they said.

P.S. Please don't hold it against these kids that they are so naive. They are just so glad to escape from abusive home lives, and they're full of the wonderful optimism of youth.

Unfortunately, they will soon learn what a dangerous, ugly, dehumanizing place the streets are. I've been praying for them ever since I left them. (By the way, because a bunch of the kids were underage, we contacted the authorities to let them know where they were — I want every available set of eyes looking after these kids!)

Chapter 15

"I ain't got no one," she said.

June, 1995

She came to our shelter for the first time almost five years ago, one of the first Covenant House kids I ever met.

From the second I saw her, I knew she was one of those kids who might not make it. Everything about her, from her tattered clothes to her slumping posture, seemed worn down. Tired. Beaten. Her eyes were two of the oldest eyes I've ever seen on a kid, smeared with pain and sadness. A smell of desperation literally clung to her clothes. I can still see her standing there....

"Hi, I'm Jessica," she mumbled that first time we met.

"I got no place to go ... can I stay here, maybe?" she said.

"I just need to rest for a couple of days," she said.

She was thirteen years old.

When she wasn't sleeping during that first visit (and she slept 18 hours that first day — most kids coming down from drugs do), we showered her with as much love and attention as we could.

Getting her clean was a full-time job in itself. It took her 30 minutes to shower away the layers of grime that first day. Picking out pants, and a shirt, and sneakers in our clothing room consumed even more time.

"I can't remember the last time I wore a pair of clean clothes," I remember her telling me. "They feel a little funny on me," she said. "I think I'll get used to it, though." A brave staff member neatly piled her old clothes, and dropped them in the trash outside.

My conversations with her? During that first visit they unwound like a springtime of disappointing weather. Every time I sensed she might open up, and I'd be able to break through to her, she would withdraw from me. The only nuggets of information she gave out, were dealt to me at her pace, and on her time.

What she shared with me was enough to scare us all to death.

"I've been on the street for two years," she said.

"I ain't got no parents. They left when I was 11," she said.

"I ain't got no one. But I can take care of myself, no problem."

For a couple of days we all loved, consoled, and comforted her.

Then, one night, she just left.

During those next few months, I couldn't get her out of my mind. I wondered where she was, how she could survive, and did anyone out there care if she lived or died (the toughest part was knowing that no one 'out there' did).

Then, out of the blue, she came back — impossibly dirty again, infinitely alone, obviously strung out and desperate for help.

We welcomed her inside. We fed her. We cleaned her up. And the next day, she left. Again.

It's been that way with Jessica for five years now.

Every few months, just when all of us have given her up for dead, Jessica comes back to us. Looking a little older than before, a little dirtier, a little more scared and alone. I've tried everything to get her to stay, but it's no use.

She *can't* stay with us. There's something inside of her now that simply won't let her stay with us.

It's not that she isn't good and decent, because Jessica is those things. It's just that the drugs and the lure of the street have swallowed Jessica whole, and become her.

As awful as it must feel for her to sleep in dumpsters and alleyways, the street has become Jessica's entire life — her home, her friend, her refuge ... her everything.

Trust in Covenant House? Sure, Jessica can do that for a couple of days, a couple of times a year. But something inside her tells Jessica she can't — she won't — she mustn't — get too close to anyone. (By the way, because Jessica was so young when she first came to Covenant House, we contacted the authorities to let them know she was with us. But Jessica always managed to leave Covenant House right before they got to meet her. She wouldn't trust *anyone*.)

To you and me, this distrust in people sounds strange. But to a girl who's been beaten and abused and abandoned by her parents (as Jessica was), her lack of faith in us is easy to understand.

Wouldn't you or I probably feel the same way?

Earlier this morning, Jessica came to us again.

It had been three months since I last saw her, and she looked awful. The youthful glow that somehow managed to cut through the layers of grime five years ago, is gone now. Her eyes, once tinged with a faint flow of hope, have long since gone blank.

She is alive, in the sense that she is still breathing in and out.

But she is barely alive. I'm really afraid this might be the last time I ever see her again (but I'm never, ever going to give up hope we will save her. Ever!).

"Hi," I said to her when she walked in this morning.

"I'm really glad to see you again," I said.

"Maybe you can stay with us awhile this time," I said, knowing the answer would probably be no.

"Yeah, maybe this time, Sister," she said. "Thanks," she said.

I'm not sure if even Jessica knows whether she'll find the faith to stay with us longer this time. I *do* know that her 'thanks' are real. As tired and beaten as she always is when she comes to Covenant House, she never, ever forgets to say 'thank you.' Ever....

We'll of course love her these next few days, because she is totally deserving of all the love we can muster. The street may own her, but a part of her is ours too. And as long as she is with us, and as long as there is a loving and caring God, there is still hope for Jessica. I know there is still hope....

Maybe you could join me in saying a prayer for her tonight? Please. I know you'd love her if you met her. She really, really is a beautiful kid. She really is....

P.S. I guess I'm stubborn (and I know I'm a natural-born optimist), but I'm never, ever going to give up on us saving Jessica. I mean, when all is said and done, Covenant House is all about hope ... hope that every kid, no matter how bad the circumstances, no matter how great the odds, will find a way to escape their horror on the street, and find a way to a long and fulfilling life.

Chapter 16

"It wasn't easy being a freak growing up."

May 1995

"I know I'm really gross and ugly," the girl with the misshaped face told me.

"I know I talk really weird, too," she slurred.

"It's not easy being like this, Sister," she said. "It's not easy."

The skinny little girl reached out and put her hand on my shoulder, and tried to smile, but it was hard to pull off. I could tell by her touch and the way she looked at me that she desperately felt like talking, and she desperately *needed* someone to just sit by and listen. Talking was her way of dealing with her hurt and sorrow and loneliness....

"I was born looking and sounding like this ... it's called Fetal Alcohol Syndrome," she slurred. "My mom was one of the world's worst alcoholics. I guess she drank a lot when she was pregnant," she said. "I guess she didn't care.

"My face was already caved in like this when I was born," she said. "I guess my mother really freaked out when she saw me," she said. "She wouldn't hold me because I was so ugly. My father didn't want me either. He ran away when I was just a little kid...."

I began to open my mouth to tell her I was sorry, but she held up her hand again, as if to tell me 'stop.' There was nothing meanspirited, or angry, or pushy in her eyes (although they were wet and hurting and dripping a little). She just wanted to talk. She needed to talk. I was very glad God had placed me before her.

"It wasn't easy being a freak growing up. The kids were always making fun of me," she said. "All the time. I never fit in. Ever. I tried to make friends, but no one ever wanted me. I think my mother hated me most of all.

"She kicked me out of the house a couple of weeks ago, right after I turned 17," she said. "She was drinking and out of it, and she said everything was my fault. Her drinking was my fault, and Dad leaving us was my fault, and her being unhappy was all my fault.

"So ... so she just locked me out of the house. I kept banging on the door to let me in, but she wouldn't. She said, 'I don't want you anymore. It's time to go. Get out.'

"I hung around for a couple of days and tried to get back in the house, but my mom never opened the door, she never went out. Finally, she left $50 under the front door and told me 'this is all I have.' That hurt so bad, Sister. So bad."

I reached out again and squeezed her shoulder, and then patted it gently. My eyes kept calling out to her, 'I'm sorry, I'm sorry, I'm sorry.' Her eyes, wet and dripping harder now, kept answering back, 'I know you are. Don't worry about me. I know you are.'

"After that, I ran into some kids in my town who said they were hitchhiking to New York," she went on. "I didn't really know them that much, but they said I could come along for the ride. They told me, 'We got jobs lined up in New York. We know people who will give you a job, too. Just help us pay for the gas, and come with us.'

"So, I went with them. The minute we got to the city, they dropped me off at a streetcorner. I still can't believe they did that to me," she said. "I ... I still can't believe ... I still...."

Joanne tried to go on, but the horror of her story finally caught up with her, and she broke down crying. I hugged her and did all I could to console her while we stood in the middle of our Intake Center. "I'm sorry, I'm sorry," I kept saying. "I'm really glad you found us," I said. "We want to help you ... I want to help you ... let us help you."

The more I told Joanne how much we cared about her, the harder she cried. If you and I had walked in her shoes, I'm sure we would have probably reacted the same way.

'Who me?' her mind must have been saying to herself. 'You want to help me? A "freak." Someone who has never been loved by anyone?' her mind kept saying to her. 'Why would you want to help me? No one wants to help me. No one!'

"We want to help you," I whispered extra loud, trying to drown out the voices of doubt raging inside her. The louder I said it, the louder she cried.

"Please help me extra hard with this one, God," I found myself saying. "Please?"

P.S. I'm not quite sure yet what's going to happen to Joanne. Please know that we are going to do all we can to help her. The first thing we absolutely, positively have to do is let her know that she is loved by us, precisely because she is good and decent and deserving of our love and her own. Your help and prayers for Joanne (and all our kids here tonight) is absolutely vital, too.

Epilogue

In a few weeks I'll mark the fifth anniversary of my coming to Covenant House. In five years of working with and loving the kids of the street, I keep thinking I've seen it all. Right now I'm thinking that I will never see anything more cruel than the way Kerri's father dropped her off on the street corner and said, "Good luck, kid." I hope I will never see anything more sad than Eric sleeping in a pipe under a bridge and waiting for his dad to come back. I can't imagine anything more brave and hopeful than the way Michelle died. And I can't imagine faith stronger than that of Diane, the girl who fills our prayer jar with notes to God.

But I also know that every time I say that to myself, "This is the saddest ... or cruelest ... or most beautiful ... story I've ever heard," I am proven wrong. I keep thinking I've seen it all, but life keeps surprising me with its horrors, and the kids keep surprising me with their courage.

These are, without a doubt, some of the saddest, cruelest, most beautiful stories I've heard in my five years here. But every day brings more children to our doorstep, each of them with a story that would shock you in one way or another. And every one of those children, just like Kerri, Eric, David, Susanna, Carol, Michelle, and Bernetta, will be asking that same question, "Does God still love me?"

I hope after reading these stories — and knowing that tonight we'll be caring for another 1,200 kids, 41,000 by the end of the year, each with just as amazing a story — that you'll want to continue to help me keep our covenant with God's kids.

Our covenant — the covenant we share with our kids — is one of the most beautiful things I've ever experienced in my life. Perhaps because it's so simple, and real, and pure.

"We're glad you found us," we say as soon as we see the kids. "We'd like to help you, if you'll let us," we say. "We'll be here, whenever you need us, 24 hours a day, 365 days a year," we tell them. "And you can always turn to us for shelter, and food, and clean clothes, and a helping hand."

"All we ask of you," we tell our kids, "is that you do your best to try to help yourself."

"We'll agree to do all we can to help you — unconditionally — as long as you make a real effort to help yourself."

It's that simple. Our covenant says that we will always be here, with the doors and our hearts open. And, standing in for our Lord above, we'll always, with hugs and patience and hope, tell the kids, "Yes! Heavens, yes! I still love you."

Thank you for reading about this covenant and agreeing to be part of it, if you can. We'd love to welcome you into this life-saving mission!

*Thousands of
kids later....*

"Dear Covenant House...."

A former kid ... 16 years later

April 5, 1995

Dear Covenant House:

Hello, my name is JoAnn ▓▓▓▓▓▓▓ I've been in Covenant House when it first opened back in the late 70's. At that time is was called "UNDER 21."

I had the best Social Worker a HURT, LOST, and LONELY teenager could have, her name is "Laura ▓▓▓▓."

Laura helped me get past my Father's death and my mother's everyday mental and physical abuse to me. If it wasn't for Covenant House-Under 21, I probably wouldn't be here today.

At the time I was at Under 21, I was 18 years old, now I'm 34 years old and I live in Washington, D.C. I work for "Family and Child Services." I'm the Administrative Secretary for "▓▓▓▓▓▓▓▓▓▓▓▓ ▓▓▓▓▓▓▓▓▓"

Anyway, when I went to Under 21, I was 18 yrs. old and had no place to go, my mother didn't want me, and my father just passed away. *I wasn't scared of the streets, I was tired of running them with no place to lay my head.* Covenant House-Under 21, took me in, fed me, and gave me hope. They helped me get on Public Assistance, which in turn gave me a place of my own (a room), and from there I went back to school for typing, and eventually I got my first full time job working in an insurance company, and I have been moving up from that point on. *Thanks to the help of Under 21.*

It's funny, 17 years ago I was living at Covenant House and here it is today, 4/5/95, 17 years later, I'm reading one of your books, "Am I Going To Heaven," and it took me back to the days of Under 21.

All I can say on paper is: Please continue helping the kids that show up at your door, a lot of us aren't really bad, we have no one to turn to, and a lot of times, we have no one to talk to and *Covenant House does make a difference.*

If at all possible, I would like to come to Covenant House and speak to the young adults that come there, and the ones that stay there. I believe in sharing my success, especially considering one of them is now using the space I once occupied. This is how I can give something back from what I learned!!

> God Bless,
> Jo Ann ▬▬▬▬

Where do we go from here?

I passionately believe the breakdown of the family unit is the single deepest ethical and moral challenge of our generation. Whether we respond to it will depend on the resolve and willingness of all of us to commit ourselves to the care and protection of family life. The time for repairing endangered families and rescuing their children is not after they have fallen apart!

The question then is ... how? How can each of us make a difference in repairing the American family? And how can we begin to make that difference now?

Because the survival of the family is so very important to our futures, we have prepared a special Family Survival Guide which can be found on the following pages. This Guide features the best things we've learned over the years working with hundreds of thousands of kids, as well as good, time-tested values that we never let ourselves forget. We hope you will share these pages with a parent you know who may need help. Thank you!

Family Survival Guide

*Reflections on
Raising Kids Today*

Values – Teaching Them in Today's World.

Communicating your values has never been more important than it is today. And the good news is, it all begins and ends with you.

When all is said and done, parents have far more influence over instilling values in their kids than any other factor.

Here are some simple, and very important, things we should all remember about values, and passing them along:

• Kids get their sense of what's right and wrong from people they love and respect. No one has more influence over teaching values than you do. Your input can make all the difference!

• When it comes to teaching values .... action *always* speaks louder than words. Kids today have a "show me" mentality. They need to see the values lived out by you. Respect for life, respect for other people, honesty, integrity ... kids get those from watching you. The old saw has never been more true ... children *do* learn what they live!

• Families are still the best vehicle for raising children. A loving, nurturing family unit, of whatever form, creates the kind of environment kids need to learn what's right and wrong ... and how to love themselves too. Values are best inculcated in an environment of love and acceptance.

• Always take time to sit and talk to your kids. Don't be afraid to say what you feel (but don't ever be too closed to listen to what your kids think).

- Always strive to teach your kids to love and respect themselves as children of God. A healthy love and respect for themselves is incredibly important for any kid. It's also the first essential step in helping a kid also learn a love and respect for those around him, and God.

- Nobody has said it better than Jesus. Those three words, "Love Thy Neighbor...." are an important message for every kid!

You've Got a Tough Job.

Most of us were never taught to be parents. So we can't help but disappoint ourselves sometimes. How often have you heard yourself using the very words you hated hearing from your own parents?

And when our kids become teenagers, it gets even harder. They seem to reject everything we've taught them. As far as they're concerned, we know nothing. Our values and beliefs are constantly challenged. Every word we utter is seen as interference. Emotions run high.

But we're more important to our teens than ever. As they try out the values of their peers, who are more influential than ever, we counter the pull of drugs and alcohol. These entangle children every day and can ruin their lives.

The Stakes Are High.

Teenagers who don't get what they need at home look elsewhere. Some run away from home. Many more consider other ways of running from pressure — a once bright and happy son escapes to drugs, a vivacious daughter starts drinking. Think about these facts:

- Each year, one million students drop out of high school or are chronically truant.
- Four out of 10 teenage girls will become pregnant before age 20.
- Although marijuana use has declined in the past years, addiction to cocaine, especially crack, has doubled.
- One in four teens develops a drinking problem during his teen years; about 10,000 will die in alcohol-related accidents this year.
- Each year, 5,000 to 6,000 teens die in suicide-related deaths, and the number is growing, one every 90 minutes. For every death, at least 100 other young people attempt suicide.

The Turbulent Teens.

Teens face many pressures that adults don't take seriously. Their bodies are changing — they have to adjust to the new person they see in the mirror. They feel different. They become interested in sex.

Self-doubt is constant. They feel pressure to conform and fear ridicule if they don't.

These changes can be bewildering, frightening and even depressing.

Teens can have remarkable insights. But they also surprise us with their lack of good judgment.

Your Teen Needs You.

At the time teenagers are crying out to be treated as adults, they also need a nurturing home, a refuge. And though they deny it passionately, they need structure, limits, lots of help sorting out their lives and most important, love.

In the turbulence of growing up, it is important for us parents to remember (even if our teens seem to forget) that we love each other. In the end, that's what makes the whole struggle worthwhile.

How Well Do You Know Your Kids?

You may say, "My teenager wouldn't do that." Most don't. But even if yours wouldn't, think about the following questions:

- Where is your child right now?
- What are your teen's deepest fears?
- Who is your son or daughter's best friend?
- Do your teen's friends feel welcome in your home?

Remember, a strong relationship with your children is the best way for you to guide them, and to prevent them from becoming a sorry statistic.

Getting Along With Your Teen.

Here are some ideas and techniques you can try to improve your relationship with your teen. If they don't work at first, keep trying. They take practice.

1. Make time for your teen. Find an activity you enjoy doing together and pursue it. If your invitations are declined, keep asking.

2. Listen, really listen. Because parents have so much to do and so little time, we often try to listen while cleaning, washing dishes or fixing the car. Put your chores aside so your teen knows you're really paying attention.

3. Take the long view. Don't treat minor mishaps as major catastrophes. Choose the important issues. Don't make your home a battleground.

4. Tolerate differences. View your teenager as an individual distinct from you. This doesn't mean you can't state your opinion if you disagree.

5. Respect your teenager's privacy. If a behavior is worrying you, speak up.

6. Let your teens sort things out themselves. Never say that you know how your teen feels. They believe their feelings (so new and personal) are unique. They'll learn otherwise — without your help. And never imply that their feelings don't matter or will change. Because teens live in the present, it doesn't matter that they'll soon feel differently.

7. Don't judge. State facts instead of opinions when

you praise or criticize. Stating facts like "Your poem made me smile," or "This report card is all Cs and Ds!" leaves it up to your teen to draw the appropriate conclusions. Teens are sensitive about being judged — positively as well as negatively.

8. Be generous with praise. Praise your child's efforts, not just accomplishments. And don't comment on the person. "You're a great artist" is hard to live up to. "I loved that drawing" is a fact and comes from your heart.

9. Set reasonable limits. Teens need them. Your rules should be consistently applied — and rooted in your deepest beliefs and values.

10. Teach your teen to make sensible decisions and choices by encouraging independence and letting your teenager make mistakes. Don't step in unless you have to.

How to Make Anger Work.

All parents get furious at their children. We can't help it. But some parents feel bad about being angry and keep quiet. Though it's easy to say things in anger that you don't mean, anger can also spark talks that will help you and your teen get to know each other better.

Some Guidelines.

• When you get mad, don't blame or accuse. Say how you *feel* — annoyed, irritated, upset, etc. —

and why. Be specific. Talk facts. Blaming only forces a teen to argue his point, arouses tempers, and kills dialogue.

- Think solution, not victory. Don't try to win arguments.

- Stick to the present incident. Fighting old battles will only aggravate a situation.

- Be careful not to attack your teen's person or character. Say, "I'm furious that you didn't clean up after the mess you made" — *not,* "You're a lazy slob!" Your son or daughter may give up trying to improve.

- If the situation is touchy, put your ideas in a letter. You can say exactly what you mean — and your teen will have time to think it over before answering.

Signs That Your Child Needs Outside Help.

- Suicidal talk of any kind. A suicidal teen may also give away valued possessions, make a will, talk about death or dying or say his family would be better off without him.

- Recent changes in sleeping or eating habits, thinking patterns, personality, friendships, study habits, activities. A sudden unexplained end to a long depression often precedes a suicide attempt. Major weight loss can be a sign of bulimia or anorexia — dangerous problems.

- Drug or alcohol use. You might notice: irrational

or irresponsible behavior, lying, secretiveness, severe mood swings, a sudden increase in accidents. A teen with a problem may have dilated pupils or wear sunglasses indoors, or complain about not sleeping or not feeling well. Valuables may disappear. You may find drug paraphernalia or alcohol containers around the house.

- A recent change in friends who you feel may be involved with drugs or alcohol may indicate that your child is involved or be a sign that your child is having other problems.

- Law-breaking behavior, even if the police and courts aren't involved. You might notice new possessions and money not accounted for.

- Poor self-image. Doubts are normal. But persistently low self-esteem is a problem.

- Serious depression. Listlessness, loneliness, withdrawal, difficulty making friends.

- Rebelliousness to the point of total, continual defiance.

- Problems at school, including class-cutting, absenteeism, a sudden drop in grades.

- Fears or anxieties that interfere with everyday activities.

- Problems between family members that aren't solved by listening and discussing. In fact, family changes such as a death, divorce or remarriage are times when teens often need some outside help.

When to Get Help For Yourself.

- Things aren't going well with your family but you can't figure out why.
- You disagree totally with positions your spouse has taken on issues concerning your teen and the two of you can't find a compromise.
- You have trouble holding a job.
- You are abusing drugs or alcohol.
- You get violent with your teenager and can't control yourself.
- Your spouse gets violent with you or your child.

What to Do If Your Teen Runs Away.

Most kids who run away return within 48 hours. Those who stay away can find themselves in many dangerous situations. So do everything you can to bring your child home.

- Keep a notebook recording steps you've taken and dates.
- Check in with: neighbors, relatives, and your teen's friends, teachers, employer or co-workers.
- Contact local hangouts and hospitals.
- Call the police. Have an officer come to your house to take a report and pick up recent photos, dental records and fingerprints if available. Get his name; badge number and phone number; the police report number; and the name of the officer who will follow up.
- Make sure the police lists your teen in the National

Crime Information Center (NCIC) to the state clearinghouse on missing children, if there is one in your state.

- Contact the National Center for Missing and Exploited Children for help with law enforcement officials — 1-800-843-5678.

- Call the Covenant House NINELINE for support and to check for messages. Leave a message. Also check with any local runaway hotlines.

- Contact runaway shelters locally and in nearby states.

- Make posters with photos of your teen, listing: age, height, weight, hair and eye color, complexion, physical characteristics (such as scars, birthmarks, braces or pierced ears), circumstances of disappearance, your phone number and police contacts. Distribute these to truck stops, youth-oriented businesses, hospitals, law-enforcement agencies.

- Be prepared for the first conversation with your teen. Whether in person or by phone, show concern, not anger. Say, "I love you."

- Prepare to quickly begin resolving the problems which caused your child to leave home. When your child returns home, emotions are likely to run high. Someone outside your family can help you all deal with these emotions. You may find that planned time for your teen in a temporary residence or shelter is necessary while you are resolving problems. So get outside help from a trained counselor.

A Call to Faith

*A Letter from a Covenant House
Community member*

"God was calling me closer and I responded...."

The following was written by
Cindy Jazwa, a member of the
Covenant House Faith Community

I don't remember exactly what possessed me the evening I decided to do some sort of volunteer work. I will never forget driving to a Cleveland Cavaliers game with my parents, announcing from the backseat, "I think I'm going to sell my business and go do some missionary work." An announcement like this took everyone by surprise, especially my brother who didn't hesitate to ask if I was feeling okay.

At the time, I was the owner of a very successful Subway Sandwich Shop. To those people around me everything seemed perfect, but I knew inside something wasn't quite right. I kept feeling there was something else I was supposed to be doing and somehow on the way to the basketball game it all clicked. All of a sudden I felt a deep burning need to help others who hadn't been as fortunate as myself.

I was getting real comfortable with the idea. I started reviewing my options and decided that Covenant House Faith Community was the place for me. When I read the basic requirements I began to wonder if my brother wasn't right and that maybe I did need my head examined. What was it that was making me want to leave my extremely comfortable lifestyle to pray twice a day, work with street kids, live communally with a bunch of strangers and make $15 a week? At the time I couldn't grasp exactly what it was but I knew one thing for sure, that I had to go check this place out.

I flew to New York City to stay with the Faith Community for a week. It was one of the most confusing weeks of my life. I had so many questions to ask and they had some for me as well. I started the week knowing this was the place for me and by the time Friday came I was ready to go home and considering volunteering somewhere else. At the end of the week I was advised to go home, relax and pray for help with my decision.

I took the advice I had been given to heart. I was so confused and I knew God was the only one that could show me the path I was to take next. I relaxed and prayed for a sign. Unfortunately, no sign dropped from the sky telling me what to do, nor did the voice of God speak to me, but gradually an unbelievable peace came over me and I knew Covenant House Faith Community was the place for me. Somehow everything was going to be okay.

It's hard for me to believe I'm getting near the end of my 13-month commitment. I've learned so much about myself, the kids and God. I've learned, for instance, that sometimes it's our own insecurities that keep us from drawing closer and listening to others. Street kids, I've come to learn, have a lot more to offer me about life than I could ever hope to teach them. I've also come to see that God moves in truly mysterious ways. Whenever I've looked to God in desperation, somehow, I've always come out of the experience with peace of mind.

I don't know yet what I will be doing at the end of my commitment, but I do know a few things for sure. For instance, I made the right decision when I joined Faith Community; God was calling me closer and I responded. It's scary not being sure of my next move, but I know that when the time comes to make that decision God will give me the gentle assurance I need. Surely, I will find compassion in my heart every time I see a homeless person. Lastly, and perhaps more importantly, I know that street kids can appear rough and undeserving, but just like you and I, they deserve to be treated with respect and love.

If you would like more information about joining the Faith Community, please write to Orientation Director of Faith Community, 346 West 17th Street, New York, NY 10011-5002, or call (212) 727-4971.

Need counseling
or support?

*Call our NINELINE counselors
at 1-800-999-9999.*

*We'll put you in touch with
people who can help you right
in your hometown.*

1-800-999-9999

This call is free.

Covenant House
346 West 17th Street
New York, NY 10011

Covenant House New Jersey
Atlantic City:
3529 Pacific Avenue
Atlantic City, NJ 08401

Newark:
14 William Street
Newark, NJ 07102

Covenant House Washington, D.C.
P.O. Box 77764
Washington, D.C. 20013

Covenant House Florida
733 Breakers Avenue
Fort Lauderdale, FL 33304

Covenant House New Orleans
611 North Rampart Street
New Orleans, LA 70112

Covenant House Alaska
609 F Street
Anchorage, AK 99501

Covenant House California
1325 N. Western Avenue
Hollywood, CA 90027

Covenant House Texas
1111 Lovett Boulevard
Houston, TX 77006

Covenant House Donor Assistance Line: 1-800-388-3888

"I bound myself by oath, I made a covenant with you ... and you became mine."
                                                              Ezekiel 16:8

The only way to stop the pain and degradation of street children is to get more people involved in solutions to the devastating problems they face every night of their lives.

After you read this book, please pass it along to a friend. If you would like more copies, just fill out this coupon and return it to us in the envelope provided. And know that because you took the time to care, a kid won't have to sell himself to survive tonight.

Please send me _____ copies of *Does God still love me?* To help defray the cost of sending you these books, we request a minimum donation of $5 per book.

Name_____

Address_____

City_____State _____ Zip_____
Please make your check payable to Covenant House.
Your gift is tax deductible.

Many people like to charge their gift. If you would like to, please fill out the information below:

I prefer to charge my: _____MasterCard _____Visa

Account # _____

Amount_____ Exp. Date _____

Signature_____

Mail to: **Covenant House**
            JAF Box 2973
            New York, NY 10116-2973

COUPON

Or, call 1-800-388-3888 to charge your gift on your MasterCard® or Visa® or to get more information.

"I bound myself by oath, I made a covenant with you ... and you became mine."

Ezekiel 16:8

Covenant House depends almost entirely on gifts from friends like you to help 41,000 homeless and runaway children every year. We provide food, clothing, shelter, medical attention, educational and vocational training, and counseling to kids with no place to go for help. Please help if you can.

YES! I want to help the kids at Covenant House.
Here is my gift of: ☐ **$10** ☐ **$20** ☐ **$25** ☐ **Other**

Name _____

Address _____

City _____ **State** _____ **Zip** _____

Please make your check payable to Covenant House.
Your gift is tax deductible.

Many people like to charge their gift. If you would like to, please fill out the information below:

I prefer to charge my: _____ **MasterCard** _____ **Visa**

Account # _____

Amount _____ **Exp. Date** _____

Signature _____

Mail to: **Covenant House**
JAF Box 2973
New York, NY 10116-2973

COUPON

Or, call 1-800-388-3888 to charge your gift.

Copies of our financial and operating reports have been filed with the state and are available on request. To obtain one, simply write: New York State Department of State, Charities Registration Section, 162 Washington Avenue, Albany, NY 12231 or Covenant House, JAF Box 2973, New York, NY 10116-2973. West Virginia residents may obtain a summary of the registration and financial documents from the Secretary of State, State Capitol, Charleston, WV 25305. A copy of the official registration and financial information may be obtained from the Pennsylvania Department of State by calling, toll free, within Pennsylvania, 1-800-732-0999. Registration does not imply endorsement. A copy of the official registration and financial information may be obtained by calling, within Florida, 1-800-435-7352. Registration and financial documents are available from the Maryland Secretary of State, State House, Annapolis, MD 21401. Registration does not imply endorsement.